MONTH:

MONDAY

TUESDAY

WEDNESDAY

THURSDAY

FRIDAY

waiting for the wheek! end

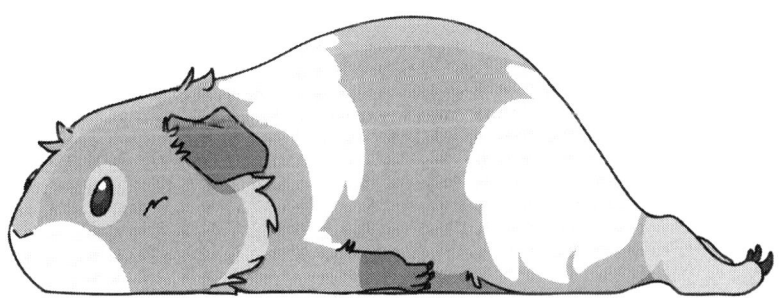

NAME: _____

CONTACT INFO: _____

WHEEK! LY SCHEDULE PLANNER
52 WEEKS - UNDATED

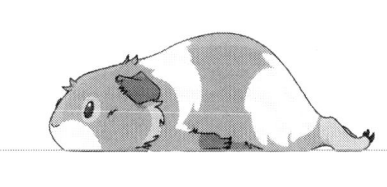

SATURDAY

[ ]

SUNDAY

[ ]

NOTES:

PRIORITIES:

TO-DO THIS WEEK:

MONTH:

MONDAY

TUESDAY

WEDNESDAY

THURSDAY

FRIDAY

SATURDAY

SUNDAY

NOTES:

PRIORITIES:

TO-DO THIS WEEK:

MONTH:

MONDAY

TUESDAY

WEDNESDAY

THURSDAY

FRIDAY

SATURDAY

SUNDAY

NOTES:

PRIORITIES:

TO-DO THIS WEEK:

MONTH:

MONDAY

TUESDAY

WEDNESDAY

THURSDAY

FRIDAY

SATURDAY

SUNDAY

NOTES:

PRIORITIES:

TO-DO THIS WEEK:

MONTH:

MONDAY

TUESDAY

WEDNESDAY

THURSDAY

FRIDAY

SATURDAY

SUNDAY

NOTES:

PRIORITIES:

TO-DO THIS WEEK:

MONTH:

MONDAY

TUESDAY

WEDNESDAY

THURSDAY

FRIDAY

SATURDAY

SUNDAY

NOTES:

PRIORITIES:

TO-DO THIS WEEK:

MONTH:

MONDAY

TUESDAY

WEDNESDAY

THURSDAY

FRIDAY

SATURDAY

SUNDAY

NOTES:

PRIORITIES:

TO-DO THIS WEEK:

MONTH:

MONDAY

TUESDAY

WEDNESDAY

THURSDAY

FRIDAY

SATURDAY

SUNDAY

NOTES:

PRIORITIES:

TO-DO THIS WEEK:

MONTH:

MONDAY

TUESDAY

WEDNESDAY

THURSDAY

FRIDAY

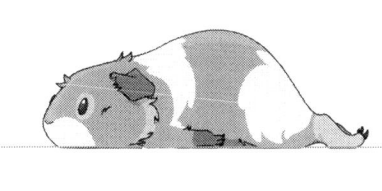

SATURDAY

SUNDAY

NOTES:

PRIORITIES:

TO-DO THIS WEEK:

MONTH:

MONDAY

TUESDAY

WEDNESDAY

THURSDAY

FRIDAY

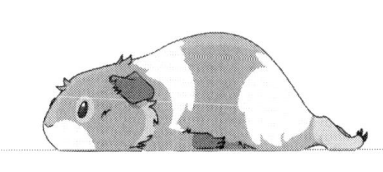

SATURDAY

SUNDAY

NOTES:

PRIORITIES:

TO-DO THIS WEEK:

MONTH:

MONDAY

TUESDAY

WEDNESDAY

THURSDAY

FRIDAY

SATURDAY

SUNDAY

NOTES:

PRIORITIES:

TO-DO THIS WEEK:

MONTH:

MONDAY

TUESDAY

WEDNESDAY

THURSDAY

FRIDAY

SATURDAY

SUNDAY

NOTES:

PRIORITIES:

TO-DO THIS WEEK:

MONTH:

MONDAY

TUESDAY

WEDNESDAY

THURSDAY

FRIDAY

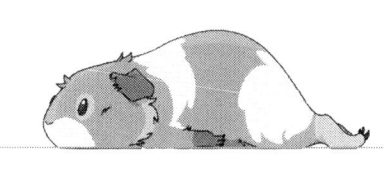

SATURDAY

SUNDAY

NOTES:

PRIORITIES:

TO-DO THIS WEEK:

MONTH:

MONDAY

TUESDAY

WEDNESDAY

THURSDAY

FRIDAY

SATURDAY

SUNDAY

NOTES:

PRIORITIES:

TO-DO THIS WEEK:

MONTH:

MONDAY

TUESDAY

WEDNESDAY

THURSDAY

FRIDAY

SATURDAY

SUNDAY

NOTES:

PRIORITIES:

TO-DO THIS WEEK:

MONTH:

MONDAY

TUESDAY

WEDNESDAY

THURSDAY

FRIDAY

SATURDAY

SUNDAY

NOTES:

PRIORITIES:

TO-DO THIS WEEK:

MONTH:

MONDAY

TUESDAY

WEDNESDAY

THURSDAY

FRIDAY

SATURDAY

SUNDAY

NOTES:

PRIORITIES:

TO-DO THIS WEEK:

MONTH:

MONDAY

TUESDAY

WEDNESDAY

THURSDAY

FRIDAY

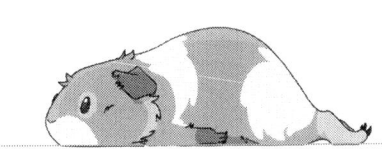

SATURDAY

SUNDAY

NOTES:

PRIORITIES:

TO-DO THIS WEEK:

MONTH:

MONDAY

TUESDAY

WEDNESDAY

THURSDAY

FRIDAY

SATURDAY

SUNDAY

NOTES:

PRIORITIES:

TO-DO THIS WEEK:

MONTH:

MONDAY

TUESDAY

WEDNESDAY

THURSDAY

FRIDAY

SATURDAY

SUNDAY

NOTES:

PRIORITIES:

TO-DO THIS WEEK:

MONTH:

MONDAY

TUESDAY

WEDNESDAY

THURSDAY

FRIDAY

SATURDAY

SUNDAY

NOTES:

PRIORITIES:

TO-DO THIS WEEK:

MONTH:

MONDAY

TUESDAY

WEDNESDAY

THURSDAY

FRIDAY

SATURDAY

SUNDAY

NOTES:

PRIORITIES:

TO-DO THIS WEEK:

MONTH:

MONDAY

TUESDAY

WEDNESDAY

THURSDAY

FRIDAY

SATURDAY

SUNDAY

NOTES:

PRIORITIES:

TO-DO THIS WEEK:

MONTH:

MONDAY

TUESDAY

WEDNESDAY

THURSDAY

FRIDAY

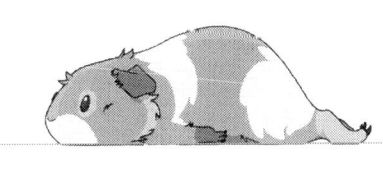

SATURDAY

SUNDAY

NOTES:

PRIORITIES:

TO-DO THIS WEEK:

MONTH:

MONDAY

TUESDAY

WEDNESDAY

THURSDAY

FRIDAY

SATURDAY

SUNDAY

NOTES:

PRIORITIES:

TO-DO THIS WEEK:

MONTH:

MONDAY

TUESDAY

WEDNESDAY

THURSDAY

FRIDAY

SATURDAY

SUNDAY

NOTES:

PRIORITIES:

TO-DO THIS WEEK:

MONTH:

MONDAY

TUESDAY

WEDNESDAY

THURSDAY

FRIDAY

SATURDAY

SUNDAY

NOTES:

PRIORITIES:

TO-DO THIS WEEK:

MONTH:

MONDAY

TUESDAY

WEDNESDAY

THURSDAY

FRIDAY

SATURDAY

SUNDAY

NOTES:

PRIORITIES:

TO-DO THIS WEEK:

MONTH:

MONDAY

TUESDAY

WEDNESDAY

THURSDAY

FRIDAY

SATURDAY

☐

SUNDAY

☐

NOTES:

PRIORITIES:

TO-DO THIS WEEK:

MONTH:

MONDAY

TUESDAY

WEDNESDAY

THURSDAY

FRIDAY

SATURDAY

SUNDAY

NOTES:

PRIORITIES:

TO-DO THIS WEEK:

MONTH:

MONDAY

TUESDAY

WEDNESDAY

THURSDAY

FRIDAY

SATURDAY

SUNDAY

NOTES:

PRIORITIES:

TO-DO THIS WEEK:

MONTH:

MONDAY

TUESDAY

WEDNESDAY

THURSDAY

FRIDAY

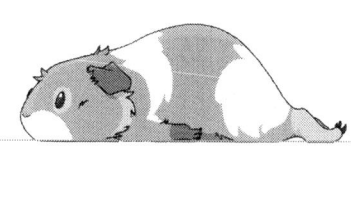

SATURDAY

SUNDAY

NOTES:

PRIORITIES:

TO-DO THIS WEEK:

MONTH:

MONDAY

TUESDAY

WEDNESDAY

THURSDAY

FRIDAY

SATURDAY

SUNDAY

NOTES:

PRIORITIES:

TO-DO THIS WEEK:

MONTH:

MONDAY

TUESDAY

WEDNESDAY

THURSDAY

FRIDAY

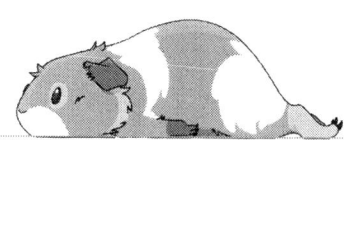

SATURDAY

SUNDAY

NOTES:

PRIORITIES:

TO-DO THIS WEEK:

MONTH:

MONDAY

TUESDAY

WEDNESDAY

THURSDAY

FRIDAY

SATURDAY

SUNDAY

NOTES:

PRIORITIES:

TO-DO THIS WEEK:

MONTH:

MONDAY

TUESDAY

WEDNESDAY

THURSDAY

FRIDAY

SATURDAY

SUNDAY

NOTES:

PRIORITIES:

TO-DO THIS WEEK:

MONTH:

MONDAY

TUESDAY

WEDNESDAY

THURSDAY

FRIDAY

SATURDAY

☐

SUNDAY

☐

NOTES:

PRIORITIES:

TO-DO THIS WEEK:

MONTH:

MONDAY

TUESDAY

WEDNESDAY

THURSDAY

FRIDAY

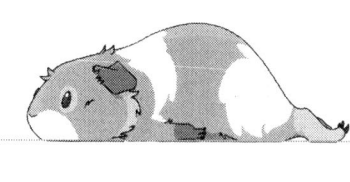

SATURDAY

SUNDAY

NOTES:

PRIORITIES:

TO-DO THIS WEEK:

MONTH:

MONDAY

TUESDAY

WEDNESDAY

THURSDAY

FRIDAY

SATURDAY

SUNDAY

NOTES:

PRIORITIES:

TO-DO THIS WEEK:

MONTH:

MONDAY

TUESDAY

WEDNESDAY

THURSDAY

FRIDAY

SATURDAY

SUNDAY

NOTES:

PRIORITIES:

TO-DO THIS WEEK:

MONTH:

MONDAY

TUESDAY

WEDNESDAY

THURSDAY

FRIDAY

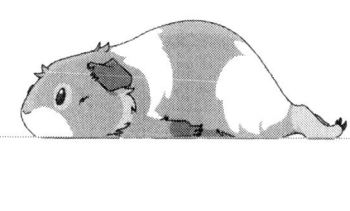

SATURDAY

SUNDAY

NOTES:

PRIORITIES:

TO-DO THIS WEEK:

MONTH:

MONDAY

TUESDAY

WEDNESDAY

THURSDAY

FRIDAY

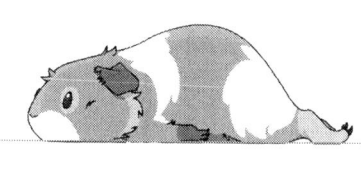

SATURDAY

SUNDAY

NOTES:

PRIORITIES:

TO-DO THIS WEEK:

MONTH:

MONDAY

TUESDAY

WEDNESDAY

THURSDAY

FRIDAY

SATURDAY

SUNDAY

NOTES:

PRIORITIES:

TO-DO THIS WEEK:

MONTH:

MONDAY

TUESDAY

WEDNESDAY

THURSDAY

FRIDAY

SATURDAY

SUNDAY

NOTES:

PRIORITIES:

TO-DO THIS WEEK:

MONTH:

MONDAY

TUESDAY

WEDNESDAY

THURSDAY

FRIDAY

SATURDAY

SUNDAY

NOTES:

PRIORITIES:

TO-DO THIS WEEK:

MONTH:

MONDAY

TUESDAY

WEDNESDAY

THURSDAY

FRIDAY

SATURDAY

SUNDAY

NOTES:

PRIORITIES:

TO-DO THIS WEEK:

MONTH:

MONDAY

TUESDAY

WEDNESDAY

THURSDAY

FRIDAY

SATURDAY

SUNDAY

NOTES:

PRIORITIES:

TO-DO THIS WEEK:

MONTH:

MONDAY

TUESDAY

WEDNESDAY

THURSDAY

FRIDAY

SATURDAY

SUNDAY

NOTES:

PRIORITIES:

TO-DO THIS WEEK:

MONTH:

MONDAY

TUESDAY

WEDNESDAY

THURSDAY

FRIDAY

SATURDAY

SUNDAY

NOTES:

PRIORITIES:

TO-DO THIS WEEK:

MONTH:

MONDAY

TUESDAY

WEDNESDAY

THURSDAY

FRIDAY

SATURDAY

SUNDAY

NOTES:

PRIORITIES:

TO-DO THIS WEEK:

MONTH:

MONDAY

TUESDAY

WEDNESDAY

THURSDAY

FRIDAY

SATURDAY

SUNDAY

NOTES:

PRIORITIES:

TO-DO THIS WEEK:

MONTH:

MONDAY

TUESDAY

WEDNESDAY

THURSDAY

FRIDAY

SATURDAY

SUNDAY

NOTES:

PRIORITIES:

TO-DO THIS WEEK:

2019

January

	Mo	Tu	We	Th	Fr	Sa	Su
1		1	2	3	4	5	6
2	7	8	9	10	11	12	13
3	14	15	16	17	18	19	20
4	21	22	23	24	25	26	27
5	28	29	30	31			

February

	Mo	Tu	We	Th	Fr	Sa	Su
5					1	2	3
6	4	5	6	7	8	9	10
7	11	12	13	14	15	16	17
8	18	19	20	21	22	23	24
9	25	26	27	28			

May

	Mo	Tu	We	Th	Fr	Sa	Su
18			1	2	3	4	5
19	6	7	8	9	10	11	12
20	13	14	15	16	17	18	19
21	20	21	22	23	24	25	26
22	27	28	29	30	31		

June

	Mo	Tu	We	Th	Fr	Sa	Su
22						1	2
23	3	4	5	6	7	8	9
24	10	11	12	13	14	15	16
25	17	18	19	20	21	22	23
26	24	25	26	27	28	29	30

September

	Mo	Tu	We	Th	Fr	Sa	Su
35							1
36	2	3	4	5	6	7	8
37	9	10	11	12	13	14	15
38	16	17	18	19	20	21	22
39	23	24	25	26	27	28	29
40	30						

October

	Mo	Tu	We	Th	Fr	Sa	Su
40		1	2	3	4	5	6
41	7	8	9	10	11	12	13
42	14	15	16	17	18	19	20
43	21	22	23	24	25	26	27
44	28	29	30	31			

2019

March

	Mo	Tu	We	Th	Fr	Sa	Su
9					1	2	3
10	4	5	6	7	8	9	10
11	11	12	13	14	15	16	17
12	18	19	20	21	22	23	24
13	25	26	27	28	29	30	31

April

	Mo	Tu	We	Th	Fr	Sa	Su
14	1	2	3	4	5	6	7
15	8	9	10	11	12	13	14
16	15	16	17	18	19	20	21
17	22	23	24	25	26	27	28
18	29	30					

July

	Mo	Tu	We	Th	Fr	Sa	Su
27	1	2	3	4	5	6	7
28	8	9	10	11	12	13	14
29	15	16	17	18	19	20	21
30	22	23	24	25	26	27	28
31	29	30	31				

August

	Mo	Tu	We	Th	Fr	Sa	Su
31				1	2	3	4
32	5	6	7	8	9	10	11
33	12	13	14	15	16	17	18
34	19	20	21	22	23	24	25
35	26	27	28	29	30	31	

November

	Mo	Tu	We	Th	Fr	Sa	Su
44					1	2	3
45	4	5	6	7	8	9	10
46	11	12	13	14	15	16	17
47	18	19	20	21	22	23	24
48	25	26	27	28	29	30	

December

	Mo	Tu	We	Th	Fr	Sa	Su
48							1
49	2	3	4	5	6	7	8
50	9	10	11	12	13	14	15
51	16	17	18	19	20	21	22
52	23	24	25	26	27	28	29
1	30	31					

2020

January

	Mo	Tu	We	Th	Fr	Sa	Su
1			1	2	3	4	5
2	6	7	8	9	10	11	12
3	13	14	15	16	17	18	19
4	20	21	22	23	24	25	26
5	27	28	29	30	31		

February

	Mo	Tu	We	Th	Fr	Sa	Su
5						1	2
6	3	4	5	6	7	8	9
7	10	11	12	13	14	15	16
8	17	18	19	20	21	22	23
9	24	25	26	27	28	29	

May

	Mo	Tu	We	Th	Fr	Sa	Su
18					1	2	3
19	4	5	6	7	8	9	10
20	11	12	13	14	15	16	17
21	18	19	20	21	22	23	24
22	25	26	27	28	29	30	31

June

	Mo	Tu	We	Th	Fr	Sa	Su
23	1	2	3	4	5	6	7
24	8	9	10	11	12	13	14
25	15	16	17	18	19	20	21
26	22	23	24	25	26	27	28
27	29	30					

September

	Mo	Tu	We	Th	Fr	Sa	Su
36		1	2	3	4	5	6
37	7	8	9	10	11	12	13
38	14	15	16	17	18	19	20
39	21	22	23	24	25	26	27
40	28	29	30				

October

	Mo	Tu	We	Th	Fr	Sa	Su
40				1	2	3	4
41	5	6	7	8	9	10	11
42	12	13	14	15	16	17	18
43	19	20	21	22	23	24	25
44	26	27	28	29	30	31	

2020

March

	Mo	Tu	We	Th	Fr	Sa	Su
9							1
10	2	3	4	5	6	7	8
11	9	10	11	12	13	14	15
12	16	17	18	19	20	21	22
13	23	24	25	26	27	28	29
14	30	31					

April

	Mo	Tu	We	Th	Fr	Sa	Su
14			1	2	3	4	5
15	6	7	8	9	10	11	12
16	13	14	15	16	17	18	19
17	20	21	22	23	24	25	26
18	27	28	29	30			

July

	Mo	Tu	We	Th	Fr	Sa	Su
27			1	2	3	4	5
28	6	7	8	9	10	11	12
29	13	14	15	16	17	18	19
30	20	21	22	23	24	25	26
31	27	28	29	30	31		

August

	Mo	Tu	We	Th	Fr	Sa	Su
31						1	2
32	3	4	5	6	7	8	9
33	10	11	12	13	14	15	16
34	17	18	19	20	21	22	23
35	24	25	26	27	28	29	30
36	31						

November

	Mo	Tu	We	Th	Fr	Sa	Su
44							1
45	2	3	4	5	6	7	8
46	9	10	11	12	13	14	15
47	16	17	18	19	20	21	22
48	23	24	25	26	27	28	29
49	30						

December

	Mo	Tu	We	Th	Fr	Sa	Su
49		1	2	3	4	5	6
50	7	8	9	10	11	12	13
51	14	15	16	17	18	19	20
52	21	22	23	24	25	26	27
1	28	29	30	31			

2021

January

	Mo	Tu	We	Th	Fr	Sa	Su
1					1	2	3
2	4	5	6	7	8	9	10
3	11	12	13	14	15	16	17
4	18	19	20	21	22	23	24
5	25	26	27	28	29	30	31

February

	Mo	Tu	We	Th	Fr	Sa	Su
5	1	2	3	4	5	6	7
6	8	9	10	11	12	13	14
7	15	16	17	18	19	20	21
8	22	23	24	25	26	27	28

May

	Mo	Tu	We	Th	Fr	Sa	Su
18						1	2
19	3	4	5	6	7	8	9
20	10	11	12	13	14	15	16
21	17	18	19	20	21	22	23
22	24	25	26	27	28	29	30
23	31						

June

	Mo	Tu	We	Th	Fr	Sa	Su
23		1	2	3	4	5	6
24	7	8	9	10	11	12	13
25	14	15	16	17	18	19	20
26	21	22	23	24	25	26	27
27	28	29	30				

September

	Mo	Tu	We	Th	Fr	Sa	Su
36			1	2	3	4	5
37	6	7	8	9	10	11	12
38	13	14	15	16	17	18	19
39	20	21	22	23	24	25	26
40	27	28	29	30			

October

	Mo	Tu	We	Th	Fr	Sa	Su
40					1	2	3
41	4	5	6	7	8	9	10
42	11	12	13	14	15	16	17
43	18	19	20	21	22	23	24
44	25	26	27	28	29	30	31

March

	Mo	Tu	We	Th	Fr	Sa	Su
9	1	2	3	4	5	6	7
10	8	9	10	11	12	13	14
11	15	16	17	18	19	20	21
12	22	23	24	25	26	27	28
13	29	30	31				

April

	Mo	Tu	We	Th	Fr	Sa	Su
14			1	2	3	4	
15	5	6	7	8	9	10	11
16	12	13	14	15	16	17	18
17	19	20	21	22	23	24	25
18	26	27	28	29	30		

July

	Mo	Tu	We	Th	Fr	Sa	Su
27				1	2	3	4
28	5	6	7	8	9	10	11
29	12	13	14	15	16	17	18
30	19	20	21	22	23	24	25
31	26	27	28	29	30	31	

August

	Mo	Tu	We	Th	Fr	Sa	Su
31							1
32	2	3	4	5	6	7	8
33	9	10	11	12	13	14	15
34	16	17	18	19	20	21	22
35	23	24	25	26	27	28	29
36	30	31					

November

	Mo	Tu	We	Th	Fr	Sa	Su
44	1	2	3	4	5	6	7
45	8	9	10	11	12	13	14
46	15	16	17	18	19	20	21
47	22	23	24	25	26	27	28
48	29	30					

December

	Mo	Tu	We	Th	Fr	Sa	Su
49			1	2	3	4	5
50	6	7	8	9	10	11	12
51	13	14	15	16	17	18	19
52	20	21	22	23	24	25	26
1	27	28	29	30	31		

waiting
for
the
wheek! end

Printed in Great
Britain
by Amazon